MW01089820

Marshallese
Alphabet

a, ā, b, d, e, i, j, k, l, ḷ, m, m̧, n, ņ, ñ, o,
o̧, ō, p, r, t, u, ū, w

Lori Phillips, EdD

PREL

Published by Pacific Resources for Education and Learning (PREL)

900 Fort Street Mall, Suite 1300 • Honolulu, Hawai'i 96813
Toll free: (1-800) 377-4773 • Phone: (808) 441-1300 • Fax: (808) 441-1385
Email: askprel@prel.org • Website: www.prel.org

BESS PRESS

Distributed by Bess Press

3565 Harding Avenue • Honolulu, Hawai'i 96816
Toll free: (1-800) 910-2377 • Phone: (808) 734-7159 • Fax: (808) 732-3627
Email: info@besspress.com • Website: www.besspress.com

Cover design by Carol Colbath

Copyright © 2004 by PREL

Library of Congress Cataloging-in-Publication Data

Marshallese alphabet / Lori Phillips.
     p. cm.
  Includes illustrations.
  ISBN 1-57306-221-9
  1. Marshallese language - Alphabet -
Juvenile literature. I. Pacific Resources
for Education and Learning. II. Title.
PL6255.P32 2004   499.5-dc21

This product was funded by the U.S. Department of Education (U.S.
ED) under the Regional Educational Laboratory program, award
number ED01CO0014. The content does not necessarily reflect the
views of the U.S. ED or any other agency of the U.S. government.

This book is part of the *Island Alphabet Books* series, which features languages and children's artwork from the U.S.-affiliated Pacific. Each book contains the complete alphabet for the language, four or five examples for each letter, and a word list with English translations. The series is published by PREL, a non-profit corporation that works collaboratively with school systems to enhance education across the Pacific.

Special thanks to the following people and organizations
for their patience and enthusiastic support of this project:
Palama Settlement ICT Learning Center
National Endowment for the Arts
Tom Barlow, Karen Ehrhorn, Kay Fukuda, Nancy Lane, Lee Noto,
Mary Dodd Pearson, and Ludwig David van Broekhuizen
of Pacific Resources for Educational and Learning (PREL)
Celina Shetana and John Sullivan of Digital Majic

This alphabet book has been reviewed by:

Cheta N. Anien, Marshallese Language Arts Specialist
Republic of the Marshall Islands Ministry of Education

Hilda Heine, PREL Scholar
Pacific Resources for Education and Learning

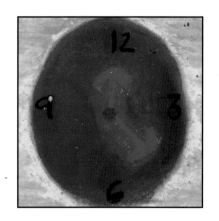

awa

addi-lep

at

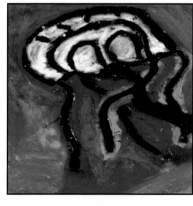

aolōk

Aa

a

āt

āne

Āā

ānbwin

bǫti

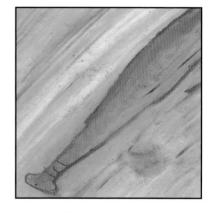

bōtta

baj

Bb

baru

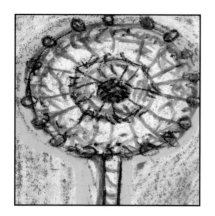

deel

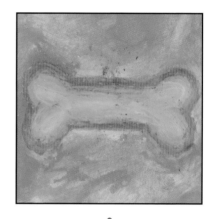

di

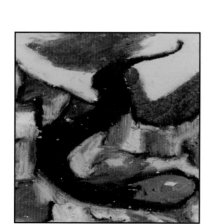

dāp

Dd

dak

eļbōn

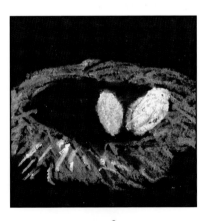

el

Ee

ek

iju

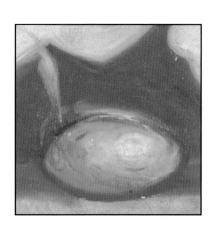

ine

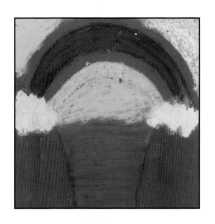

iia

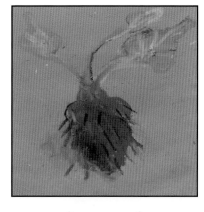

iaraj

Ii

iep

jibōr

jijej

jaam

jidpān

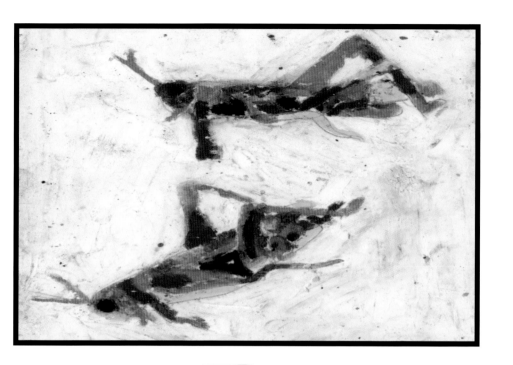

Jj

jeļo

kwōdeak

kweet

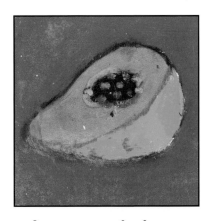

keinabbu

kidu

Kk

kōrkōr

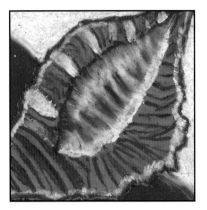

libbukwe

leta

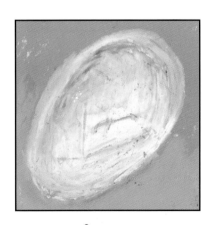

lep

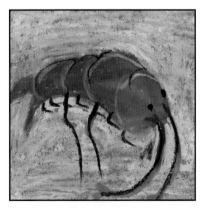

libūŋōj

Ll

limakaak

ḷae

ḷalim jen

ḷoḷḷe

إِلَّا

إِaddik

mañko

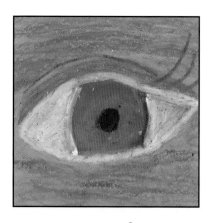

mej

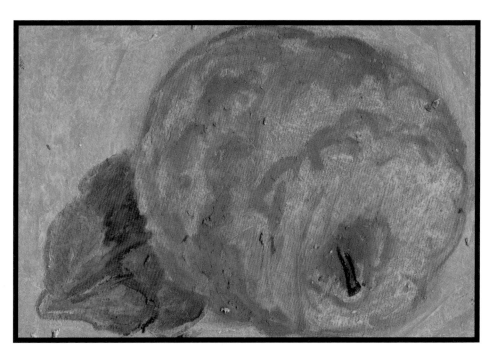

Mm

mā

m̦ade

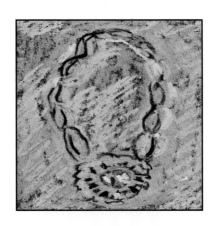

m̦arm̦ar

M̧m̧

m̧aj

ni

niitōḽ

niñniñ

Nn

ni kenato

ŋam

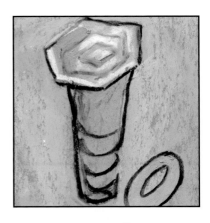

ŋat

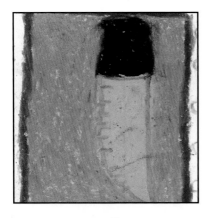

ŋaip

Ṇ ṇ
ṇo

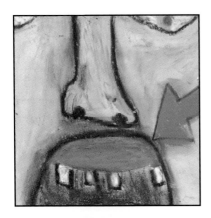

ñad

ñiñat

ñōl

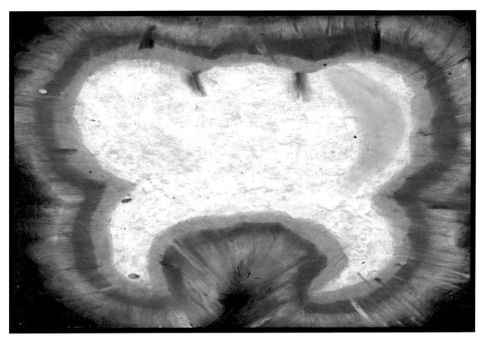

Ññ
ñi

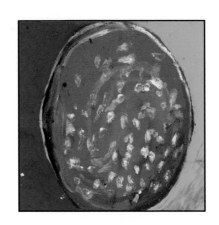

oran

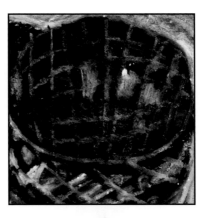

ok

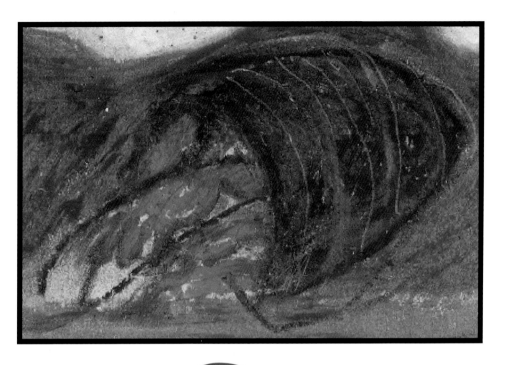

Oo

om

ọọ

ọkwōn

Oo

ﻮﻗ

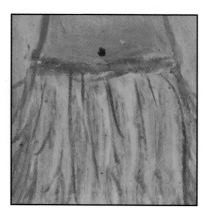

ōr

Ōō

ōn

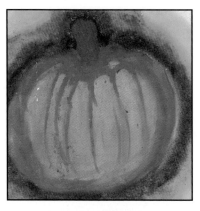

paañke

peinabōl

pako

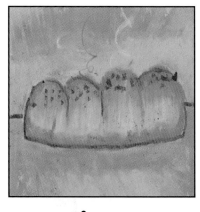

pilawe

Pp

pinana

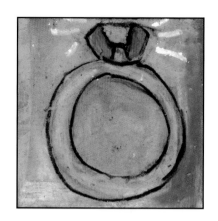

riiñ

rooj

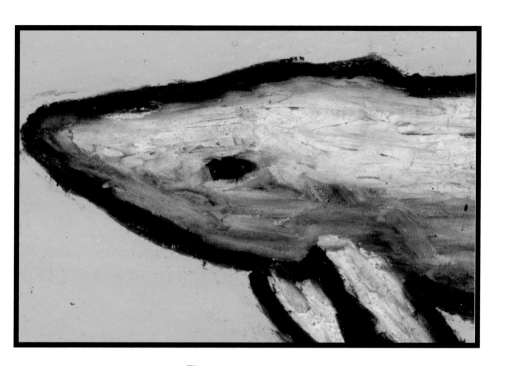

Rr

raj

take

tōreej

taij

Tt

tol

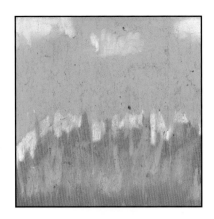

ujooj

uɯ̃

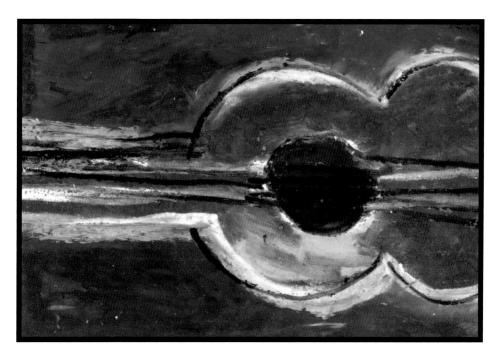

Uu

ukulele

ūl

Ūū

ūlūl

wōd

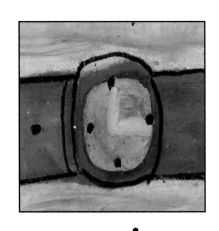

waj

Ww

wōn

English Translations

addi-lep	toe
aḷ	sun
aolōk	jellyfish
at	hat
awa	clock
ānbwin	skinny man
āne	island
āt	eyebrow
baj	bus
baru	crab
bọti	nose
bōtta	bat
dak	duck
dāp	eel
deel	fan
di	bone
ek	fish
el	nest

eḷbōn	elephant
iaraj	taro
iep	basket
iia	rainbow
iju	star
ine	sprouting coconut
jaam	jam
jeḷo	cricket
jibōr	zipper
jidpān	saw
jijej	scissors
keinabbu	papaya
kidu	dog
kōrkōr	canoe
kweet	octopus
kwōdeak	mustache
lep	egg
leta	letter
libbukwe	shell
libūŋōj	shrimp

limakaak	kite
l̩addik	boy
l̩ae	calm
l̩alim jen	nickel
l̩ol̩le	lollipop
mañko	mango
mā	breadfruit
mej	eye
m̩ade	spear
m̩aj	worm
m̩arm̩ar	shell necklace
ni	coconut
ni kenato	coconut tree
niitōl̩	needle
niññiñ	baby
ŋaip	knife
ŋam	mosquito
ŋat	bolt
ŋo	wave
ñad	gum

ñi	tooth
ñiñat	false teeth
ñōl	top of wave
ok	fishing net
om	hermit crab
oran	orange
o̧kwōn	organ
o̧o̧	circle
o̧o̧j	horse
ōn	vitamins
ōr	grass skirt
paañke	pumpkin
pako	shark
peinabōl	pineapple
pilawe	bread
pinana	banana
raj	whale
riiñ	ring
rooj	rose
taij	dice

take	turkey
toḷ	mountain
tōreej	thread
ujooj	grass
ukulele	ukulele
uṃ	underground oven
ūl	dorsal fin
ūlūl	axe
waj	watch
wōd	coral
wōn	turtle